© Aladdin Books Ltd 1990

First published in 1990
in the United States by
Gloucester Press Inc.
387 Park Avenue South
New York NY 10016

ISBN 0-531-17208-2

Library of Congress Catalog Number: 89-81603

Printed in Belgium

The author, Tim Lobstein PhD, *is author of* Children's Food *and* Fast Food Facts. *He is also co-editor of the Food Magazine.*

Design: Rob Hillier, Andy Wilkinson
Editor: Margaret Fagan
Picture researcher: Cecilia Weston-Baker
Illustrator: Ron Hayward Associates

Contents

POISONED FOOD ?

TIM LOBSTEIN

Illustrated by
Ron Hayward Associates

Gloucester Press

New York : London : Toronto : Sydney

Food in the news

Suddenly, food is in the news. Newspaper headlines describe a variety of hazards caused by eating contaminated food. Dirty food may contain germs that make us ill and food poisoning due to bacteria now affects thousands of people each year. Farm crops are sprayed with chemicals to kill weeds, but the same chemicals may be harmful to us. Some are suspected of causing cancer in children. Colorful additives in food may tempt us as we stroll past the supermarket shelves, but what do they do for our health? Today, there is an outcry about the state of the food we eat and the short-term problems caused by "poisoned food."

▷ Raw meat must be kept frozen in cold-storage warehouses to stop germs breeding. The number of reported cases of food poisoning is rising.

Many claim that the extent of short-term food problems is hardly known and needs to be more carefully investigated. Yet resources for research into food safety are limited. In the long-term our diet is also important; fatty and sugary foods affect the health of many millions of people each year. In the United States, 36 percent of the population will die of heart disease, and the majority of these deaths is now believed to be the result of eating too much fatty food. Tooth decay affects six children in every ten, largely due to eating sugary food.

Whether food makes us ill or healthy depends on what it contains and the way it is grown, processed and stored. This book will look at how modern food is made and the problems that can arise due to food poisoning and diet.

Salmonella outbreak passes 300

Glass found in tins of HP baked beans

Salmonella 'in 60% of broiler chickens'

Big business

Problems of starvation have nearly vanished in modern industrialized countries. Abundant food supplies fill the shops and most people could have a healthy diet. Diseases associated with malnutrition, which were still seen in industrialized countries until the 1940s, have almost disappeared.

In order to produce food on a large-scale, farms in industrial countries have become industries themselves. Machines have replaced human labor in the fields, and now chemicals are replacing both machines and humans. Every day massive quantities of food are moved along sophisticated transport networks to reach the stores. The world's largest companies are those that can supply farms with high tech machinery and agrochemicals, as well as transport, process and sell food.

Food is big business throughout the world but only abundantly available to some. For example, Brazil is a major exporter of frozen chickens and oranges, while many of its own people are malnourished. The only way some countries can pay for expensive imports like petrol and industrial equipment is to sell food for export. These countries grow crops for cash, while their own people may starve. Ethiopia exported food throughout its famine.

▽ During the 1930s, in Europe and the United States, many people were too poor to buy enough food, and came to soup kitchens which offered free food. The one in this photograph was in the United States.

Today industrially-developed countries have virtually abolished hunger among their own population.

The mass production of food has made some kinds of food cheaper and more widely available. But is this cheap food solely beneficial? Sugar used to be a luxury and was rarely eaten. Meat was once expensive and less fatty. Now sugar and fatty meat provide a large proportion of our modern diet. Wholegrains, beans and legumes, fish and vegetables, which are essential to a healthy diet, are eaten less often.

Multinational companies have an interest in seeing that we keep on eating mass-produced and processed foods. The oil and chemical companies (makers of pesticides) have an interest in seeing big farms continue their intensive farming. Supermarket chains and fast-food companies sell the processed products of this farming.

The world's largest food manufacturing company sells over $25,000,000,000 worth of products annually, more than the entire domestic economies of developing countries Mozambique, Nicaragua, Zambia, Haiti, Ethiopia, Jamaica, and Botswana combined.

▽ The dawning of the supermarket age saw a large number of food products in one shop, and shoppers were encouraged to help themselves. Now we buy three-quarters of all our food in supermarkets. Much of this food has been treated so it stores well and can stay on the shelf for a long period.

The perfect crop

In order to produce greater quantities of food from their land, farmers turned to technology. They uprooted bushes and trees from their fields so they could use larger machines which could plant and treat huge areas of crops. Farmers plant seeds which have been genetically selected to increase the crop yield. The seeds then get a boost of fertilizer before being dropped in the soil, and the soil may have a series of chemical treatments to increase fertility and kill bugs. As the seedlings grow they may be sprayed several times to kill insects and weeds.

After harvesting, the crop will be stored in warehouses where it may receive more chemical treatments to stop mold and prevent sprouting. The effect of all this intensive farming is to create a bumper-sized harvest of a disease-free crop for the food processing companies and supermarkets...but this type of farming can produce unwanted side effects which may affect our health.

Pesticide sprays help the farmer keep the crop free from damage or disease by destroying fungus molds (fungicides), insects (insecticides) and unwanted weeds (herbicides). They may be either systemic or contact-acting chemicals. Contact pesticides act on the pest or the plant. Systemic pesticides are absorbed into the plant. When it comes to removing leftover residues on our food, contact pesticides may be largely removed by washing or peeling. Systemic pesticides cannot be removed since they are found throughout the food.

Some of the spray-on chemicals are still in the food when we eat it. Chemicals used to kill pests on plant crops and to regulate the growth of the crops can cause allergies, birth defects and tumors in laboratory animals and are strongly suspected of being harmful to humans.

Wildlife has also been affected by intensive farming – many species have lost their natural habitat and their numbers have been drastically reduced. In some places the soil has been overused and has lost its ability to provide nutrients for growing plants without further chemical treatments and fertilizers.

▽ Huge fields sprayed from the air may grow several crops in a year. This intensive farming of plants brings us more food, but it may do so at the cost of our health. Chemicals, such as Alar which is sprayed on apples as a pesticide, are suspected of causing cancer in monkeys and rats.

Apple trees may be sprayed with growth-regulating chemicals to ensure that the fruit are a uniform size and color, and that they all ripen at the same time. Supermarkets claim shoppers prefer these "perfect" fruits which are also cheaper than fruit grown without chemicals.

Battery hens are kept in restricting cages. Infections may come from their feed (which can include "recycled" chicken carcasses), and once present, may spread easily to neighboring birds.

1. Meat infected with salmonella causes food poisoning. A chicken may eat salmonella-infected feed.

2. Unhygienic slaughtering equipment may easily pass infection to many other chicken carcasses.

3. Bacteria lie dormant in frozen meat, but multiply rapidly at room temperature, and so cause a hazard.

Fast breeding farms

Most of the meat and eggs we buy from supermarkets is also produced by intensive farming. This allows farmers to keep huge numbers of livestock more cheaply and so keeps prices down in the shops. But where animals or birds are farmed intensively they are kept tightly-packed together and, without adequate precautions, this may easily spread infection. The original source of infection may be unhygienic animal feed. This can include floor litter from intensive chicken farming. Salmonella, a bacteria commonly found in eggs and poultry, is thought to be passed on in contaminated feed.

In Britain, a brain disease has spread to cattle because the cattle feed contained infected sheep brains. There are fears that the disease (bovine spongiform encephalopathy, BSE) may spread to humans; some countries refuse to import beef from Britain because of the risk. An outbreak of another disease, botulism (which is deadly to humans), was caused by the cattle feed containing infected feathers and carcasses from a chicken farm. To increase the value of their flocks and herds, farmers breed animals and birds to weigh as much as possible. They may use hormones to boost weight and antibiotics to prevent illness. But hormone and antibiotic residues may also affect our health.

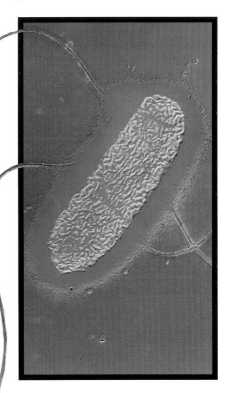

▽ Salmonella bacteria (photographed here) and another bacteria, Campylobacter, are the commonest causes of food poisoning. They can cause severe diarrhea in a healthy adult and more serious symptoms in babies, old people or those already unwell. In a few cases, salmonella poisoning is fatal.Food poisoning due to salmonella affects thousands of people every year.

4. Heating above 350°F destroys the bacteria. For this reason all meat must be properly cooked or reheated.

5. Cooked meat can be reinfected from raw meat or dirty hands which still carry the bacteria.

6. If you have salmonella symptoms, diarrhea and vomiting 12-36 hours after eating, consult a doctor.

Modern meat

When livestock arrives at the slaughterhouse, great care has to be taken to ensure that the animals are slaughtered in hygienic conditions. With hundreds of birds or animals being slaughtered each hour, it can be difficult to detect an infected carcass — infected chickens, for example, may show no symptoms, yet 60 percent of those on sale contain salmonella.

Unhygienic slaughtering can spread food poisoning bacteria. Contaminated equipment will pass bacteria to many more carcasses along the line before a problem is noticed.

▽ Care should be taken to avoid contaminating carcass meat with feces rich in bacteria. Meat hygiene inspectors may also check the buckets of offal — liver, heart, intestines — for signs of diseased animals. Inspectors have reported that meat and offal are occasionally packed into containers while still warm, and dirty with feces. Such slack hygiene leads to outbreaks of food poisoning.

Meat pies, cold cuts, sausages, salami and other similar products use the parts of an animal's carcass that are not usually saleable as raw meat. They may contain offal, skin, gristle and "mechanically recovered meat" which is produced by scraping the skeleton to produce a grey paste.

To make meat products more attractive, manufacturers need to use various additives – texturizers, flavoring agents and colors – and some of these are thought to be harmful to health. Monosodium glutamate is often used to "enhance" the taste of meat products, but it can cause adverse reactions in some people. Various meat coloring agents may cause asthma, skin rashes and hyperactivity. Reheated meat pies are one of the most common sources of food poisoning.

Mechanically recovered meat provides a good home for food poisoning bacteria and great care needs to be taken to ensure the meat is handled safely. Some consumer groups are calling for the use of this substitute for "real" meat to be clearly declared on product labels.

Butchers may sell the red meat over the counter – but where does all the fat go? Much of it may be going into meat products like sausages and pies. Regulations in Britain allow less than 30 percent lean meat in a beef sausage, but permit much greater amounts of fat. The fat may well be colored with red dye to look like lean meat. Some of the color and flavorings used may be harmful to health.

▽ One batch of sausage mix will fill a lot of sausages. To reduce contamination in mass produced meat, a manufacturer will add chemicals like sulfites which prevent bacterial growth. The sausage can be sold weeks after it is made. But some people suffer allergic reactions to sulfites.

Cheap and cheerful

During the last 30 years there has been a dramatic rise in the amount of processed foods we eat. Over two thirds of our shopping bill is spent on processed foods and this is causing concern among nutritionists. Processed foods have often lost some of the nutritional value of their original ingredients, but they may have gained in the concentration of energy. Indeed they may provide all the day's energy requirements in just one packet, but without providing the vitamins and minerals which are also needed to keep healthy. Both sugar and fat – the main ingredients of processed food – are high-energy, low-nutrient food ingredients.

Foods rich in sugar and fat need to be balanced with large amounts of high-nutrient, low-energy food like fruit, vegetables and wholegrains. However, food manufacturers make more profit selling a small amount of meat or vegetables in a sauce, or fruit-flavoured desserts or cookies than if they sold fresh food.

There are nearly 4,000 different additives available to help companies sell processed food. Emulsifiers can mix fat and water and air to make mayonnaise, ice cream, milk shakes or non-drip paint. Flavorings can boost a dull food and hide the fact it may be largely water or fat. Colorings put back lost color, or add color that was never there before, making lard look like lean meat, or water look like fruit juice. Preservatives stop colors fading and, by stopping natural decay, can keep a product fresh-looking for months, or even years.

▽ Most sugar is refined and used in candy and chocolate, ice cream, cakes and soft drinks. The sweetness, along with the flavorings and colorings, may be tempting but the nutritional value is usually very low.

Manufacturers of processed foods buy the raw ingredients very cheaply; sugar, fat and refined flour can all be produced by intensive farming. Manufacturers then use a vast range of chemical additives (the colorings and flavorings which make a dull food seem interesting), and mechanical processing techniques to turn their raw ingredients into something to sell. Finally, sophisticated packaging and advertising make their products seem even more desirable.

The problem is that cheap ingredients and additives are not particularly beneficial to our health. Some additives are under suspicion of producing harmful side effects. They have been found to provoke asthma, eczema (a skin complaint) and other allergic reactions, and some are thought to affect behavior and make children hyperactive. Additives also encourage many of us, especially children, to be attracted toward just those sweet and fatty foods we ought to avoid.

▽ Most children prefer sweet and brightly-colored food to saltier snacks. Perhaps this fact was once important as it steered early man to eat fresh fruit – a good source of nourishment. Today, sweetness is usually added to food by the sugar industry and colors by the chemical industry. Many fruit drinks gain their taste solely from added flavoring. Nutritionally, a glass of fresh water might be healthier!

Read the label

With so much of today's food produced in the factory, and with so many ingredients added, labeling has become vital. Often the only clues to the contents of processed foods are written on the label. The big print usually states the name and type of product. The small print includes a list of ingredients, the main ones first, and perhaps some information about the nutrients in the package. The chemical compounds which have been added to give the product its taste and appearance regularly appear at the bottom of the list. The label will not include information about any residues left from farming and storage, like antibiotics, insecticides or fungicides.

△ Words like *country* or *classic* may just be marketing gimmicks, and the food really comes from factories like the one above. Words like *extra* and *premium* have no legal meaning. Words like *natural*, *healthy*, and phrases like *high fiber* or *reduced sugar* are also without legal status.

△ "Pure orange juice" may mean concentrated, shipped, reconstituted and pasteurized. The production of orange juice is a large-scale industrial process. The "juice" usually arrives in a tanker as a concentrate.

Manufacturers are also required to safeguard the quality of the food they sell by indicating how fresh the food is, and how long they think it should keep before spoiling. This information can help us to avoid eating contaminated food. Packages must have a "sell by," "best before" or "consume by" date clearly printed on the label. If the store is trying to sell outdated produce, this may indicate fresh supplies are not being delivered very often. If the package says the food should be refrigerated, check to see that the store is keeping it properly chilled in a cold display cabinet or a refrigerator.

Finally, check to see that the food is packaged properly as well as labeled clearly. Packaging which is damaged could be a sign of old stock, but it could also indicate that the product has been interfered or tampered with. There have been cases of glass, screws, and other dangerous objects being found in canned and bottled food, including baby food.

The more processed a food, the longer the list of ingredients on the packet and some of these can be quite unusual; red coloring made from cactus beetles (cochineal) or cold tar (carmoisine); thickeners made from seaweed (carrageenan); glaze made from caterpillar saliva (shellac); or emulsifiers made from tree resin (guar gum and tragacanth). Some of these additives will be given as coded numbers, others by long chemical names. Some, like petroleum jelly which is used as a lubricant to prevent sticking in baking and confectionary, may not be declared at all.

For most people, most ingredients are safe, but some may react badly to certain additives and there is very little testing of additive mixtures.

Chilling facts

Listeria bacteria (photographed here) can multiply at temperatures a few degrees above freezing point. This can cause hygiene problems for food stored at low temperatures for long periods.

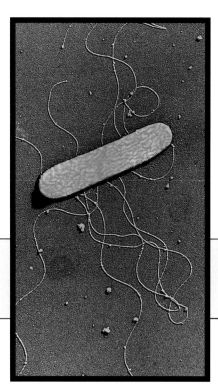

Mass-produced chilled foods are popular because they offer quality menu-meals without the need to spend hours in the kitchen.

In theory, cooking food and then storing it just above freezing point should allow it to be kept for many days before being eaten. The bacteria should be killed by the cooking and any remaining should be kept inactive by the low temperature of the refrigerator. But some bacteria, including *Listeria monocytogenes*, are able to multiply at low temperatures. Listeria contamination has been found in a variety of chilled foods including margarine, soft cheeses, chilled salads and ready-cooked meals. Food poisoning from listeria contamination is not common, but when it occurs it can be fatal.

1. Listeria poisoning is uncommon. The bacteria may be found on unwashed vegetables and raw meat.

2. The bacteria lies dormant in frozen food, but it can rapidly multiply in refrigerated and chilled foods.

◁ Keeping fish packed in ice helps keep it fresh without many hazards. Factory ships are able to catch and fully freeze fish without returning to port for weeks. But polluted seawater is contaminating some of the fish we eat with toxic chemicals. Overfishing is also leading to concern that a major food resource will become exhausted. A nutritious food may soon be lost to us.

3. Cooking to 350°F destroys listeria bacteria. Precooked food should be reheated thoroughly.

4. Foods kept chilled for long periods and not cooked – for example, soft cheeses – can be a hazard.

5. Flu-like symptoms may develop many days after the infected food has been eaten. They can cause death.

◁ Convenience foods are a home to listeria. Raw, prepared salads are a particular hazard and these are not reheated to kill off any bacteria present. Of 115 cases of listeriosis in pregnant women in Britain, there were 11 miscarriages, nine stillbirths and six neonatal deaths.

Pregnant women and people unable to cope with infections, like the old or infirm, should avoid any risk of listeria infection. As many as a third of listeria patients may die.

A study of the diets of 154 patients suffering from listeriosis in the United States found that just two foods were responsible for 20 percent of the risk: undercooked chicken and undercooked hotdogs. In Britain, over half of a sample of raw chickens was found to be contaminated. A quarter of ready-cooked convenience meals that were tested was also contaminated.

Irradiated food

All foods can eventually spoil and become poisonous to the human body. Throwing away the food which has deteriorated due to natural ageing causes huge financial losses to food producers and manufacturers. But contaminated food can now be "cleaned" using nuclear technology. Instead of fumigating warehouses with chemical pesticides, the crops can be put in front of a radioactive material and the irradiation will kill any bugs, bacteria or mold. Irradiating fruit, vegetables or grains will also slow down their ripening and sprouting, so they will last far longer and still look fresh.

△ Irradiating wheat kills insect pests, but it also destroys the valuable vitamin B1. There is evidence that monkeys and rats fed irradiated wheat can develop chromosome defects. The United States, Soviet Union and Canada already permit wheat irradiation.

◁ Irradiated food is not the same as food contaminated by fallout of the sort that followed the nuclear disaster at Chernobyl in 1986. Food contaminated with fallout is a hazard because it contains radioactive material. Irradiated food contains no radioactive material, unless very high doses of radiation are used.

Critics are worried that the irradiation technique can be used to cover up poor hygienic practices: food that has spoiled can be sterilized with irradiation and resold. Wheat containing mouse droppings or insects can be "cleaned up" and sent to be milled. Chicken meat infected with the bacteria salmonella can be irradiated and sent to supermarkets as "fresh." Contaminated foods, like shellfish, could be cleaned up by irradiation so they can pass through food safety controls. There is also a loss of vitamins when food is irradiated. Fruit may appear fresh, but irradiation combined with longer storage leads to less nutritional value. But the food industry says irradiation will lead to fewer preservatives in our food.

Consumer groups argue that good food does not need irradiating. Irradiation is, they say, a license for poor hygiene. At the very least, foods that have been irradiated should be labeled so shoppers can avoid buying them if they wish.

▽ Exposing food to radioactive materials has been going on for decades. When it is licensed for general use the process is automated, with conveyor belts taking food into the irradiator.

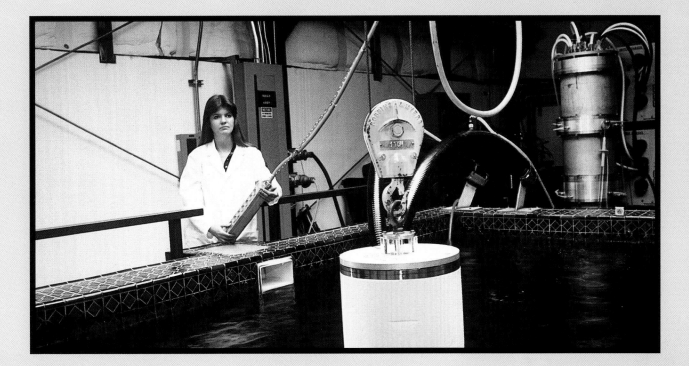

A thousand dinners a day

Catering for large numbers raises special problems of hygiene and there are many outbreaks of food poisoning which can be traced back to dirty kitchens. There is nothing that pests – cockroaches, rats and bacteria – like better than a warm, damp kitchen with dark corners and unwashed surfaces. People handling food have to pay attention to their own hygiene too – unwashed hands can spread infection to food and so can slack practices, like using the same knife on raw meat and then cooked meat.

Healthy eating also requires a varied menu. Religious and cultural needs and special dietary needs – for diabetics, for example – may have to be catered to. But the food served in a cafeteria or restaurant does not have details about the ingredients being used, so customers have no way of checking which additives have been used. There may be asthma-provoking additives in the frankfurters, for example, or excessive sugar in a pudding or animal fat in the ice cream.

Checking for poor hygiene is the responsibility of local food inspectors. They may prosecute the offending food service, and in certain conditions, can close a dirty kitchen. Small restaurants and take outs also have their problems. Many are not inspected often enough to safeguard the quality of the food they serve. If you think you have food poisoning tell your doctor and your local food inspectors – they can investigate if others were poisoned from the same source.

◁ Airline catering presents special problems. Food must be prepared, chilled and transported to the aircraft where it may not be served for many hours. In some cases the food for the return flight is also carried on board. Any accidental warming of the food can present a food poisoning hazard. Cook-chill foods have also been introduced into hospitals. But invalids are among those most vulnerable to food poisoning.

New techniques of food preparation for large-scale food services have opened up more potential hazards to consumers. Preparing food several days in advance using cook-chill technology can save on labor and avoids the rush to prepare everything fresh on the day. This saves on money and overtime. But how is the food to be kept before serving? The original intention was that cook-chilled food need only be reheated to make it palatable. But poor hygiene may leave cook-chilled food contaminated with bacteria that multiply at low temperatures. Food should be recooked to kill any bacteria — impossible in the case of salads and foods designed to be eaten cold.

Waste food is a magnet for pests. The back of a restaurant may hint at the state of the kitchens, but even clean trash cans hide pests.

△ Kitchen pests spread bacteria. Anywhere from the local corner cafe to a large institution's cafeteria can provide a breeding ground for insects, rodents and even birds. But kitchen hygiene costs money and time.

Fast food

Cattle-rearing can take up a lot of space, and in Central and South America large tracts of native forest have been destroyed to make way for beef ranches. The ranches sell most of their beef to fast-food companies – who also own land in these areas. These lost forests and their wildlife may never be replaced.

In just two or three decades there has been an enormous change in our eating habits, led by the big fast-food companies that now operate around the world. One company alone has an average of over 13,000 customers worldwide every minute, 24 hours each day, every day of the year. The burgers they have sold, if lined up side by side, would circle the earth over 100 times!

The secret of fast-food service is to have a small range of popular food, which can be cooked quickly and which is of uniform quality so the customer always knows what to expect. The atmosphere is bright and cheerful and designed to appeal to youngsters. A ploy of the fast-food business is to have few seats, and then only hard ones – alright for resting on, but not too comfortable. The food is designed to be eaten fast, too. If it stands for more than ten minutes after cooking it should be thrown away. It loses its appeal, the milkshake begins to go flat and the french fries get soft.

The trouble with the fast-food menu featuring meat and fried food is the poor nutrition it offers. Fast-food diets tend to be high in fat, salt and sugar – all ingredients that can increase the risk of a heart attack. Some fast foods also rely on additives to increase their appeal – additives that may not be listed on any label.

In their favor, big fast-food companies offer better cleanliness and standard of hygiene. The risk of poisoning from the food they serve is also slight since the food is either deep-fried or grilled, and not held warm for long periods of time.

Fast food served in other outlets, like snack bars and cafes, is often kept for longer periods in hot boxes. Unless these are kept piping hot, and many are only lukewarm, bugs quickly multiply.

▽ The fast-food industry uses thousands of tons of packaging for take out food. This does not quickly rot away and it cannot be reused. The industry is wasteful in other ways: it takes as much as 20lbs of grain used as animal feed to make just one pound of meat.

Fast-food companies offer a standard service throughout their food chains. Kentucky was the first company to open in mainland China.

Home hazards

◁ The refrigerator has liberated us from frequent shopping trips and many households only shop once a week. A well-stocked fridge holds a tempting variety of chilled foods. But variety can mean cross-contamination, raw meat in contact with cooked meat or dripping onto food below.

Although many cases of food poisoning are due to poor hygiene in the food industry, some purchased food is contaminated in the home. However, consumer groups are concerned that domestic cooking should not take the entire blame for the rising numbers of food poisoning outbreaks. Every kitchen harbors a multitude of bacteria that can spoil food and also cause food poisoning. Food bought from the store may well carry some bacteria, and the containers and implements used in every kitchen will carry some more. To avoid food spoilage and food poisoning at home, precautions have to be taken. Most forms of cooking will kill dangerous bacteria and the food is then safe to eat. Unless, that is, it is left around after cooking, and particularly if it comes into contact with uncooked food. Then it may pick up more bacteria and become a possible hazard. This is called cross-contamination.

The use of microwave ovens may also add to the increasing number of cases of food poisoning because it heats the food unevenly. "Cold spots" can leave parts of the food uncooked (or not properly reheated in the case of precooked or cook-chill food). This means that bacteria in the food may not be killed by heating.

Microwave ovens offer convenient cooking. But they leave "cold spots" in the food so it needs to be stirred. Cooking continues during the "standing time" after the oven is turned off. During this time more bacteria are being killed off.

Take it back!

Points to watch out for while shopping:
* check the sell by and best before dates on the packages.
* avoid dented cans or damaged packages.
* check that food from refrigerated cabinets feels really cold.
* Try to ensure take out foods and meals eaten out are freshly made and look (and smell) fresh – if in doubt don't risk it!

The competitive food industry fights for consumers' attention by offering more apparent choice, more foods from exotic countries, new forms of convenience foods, special "health" foods and more exciting "eating experiences." But the industry's interest in gaining a market does not always coincide with the consumers' need to eat food which is nutritious and healthy, economical and fun. Consumers have to keep voicing their views on healthy food.

If you think you have been sold something that does not have the quality that you wanted, then you should take it back to the store. If the food sold to you is unfit for humans to eat, then you have a right to complain.

△ Many shoppers choose their food to cut down health risks. Health insurance companies have been aware of the risks for a long time: they charge a higher premium to fat people because illness is more common when a person is overweight.

The quality of your life depends on the quality of the food you eat. What food producers – from farm, to factory, to supermarket – try to sell may not be what you need to buy to keep you healthy.

As a food consumer you need to take care, you need to find out what eating healthily means. You need to ignore the large print and look carefully at the small print. And you need to make a complaint if necessary.

Fresh fruit and vegetables may take longer to prepare than convenience foods, but their nutritional value is higher. Some crops are now grown "organically" – this means that as they are grown without the use of mineral fertilizers or pesticides, they are free of harmful residues and other problems due to chemicals used in farming. But this produce may be more expensive to buy.

Food facts

All shoppers have a right to complain about any product which they find to be unsatisfactory:
* It is always worth complaining to the management if you are unhappy with what they are selling. Good managers want to know about problems before they affect too many people and ruin their trade, so you are doing them a favor and future customers too.
* It is worth writing letters to companies about their products. They too want information about how their products are received.
* Refer anything serious to your local state authority: they uphold the law and have food inspectors who are the "police force" controlling the industry.
* Get involved with your school cafeteria facilities: talk to the staff responsible about what they are doing and what you would like to see being done.
* Find out about the food policies your local government and national government have. Are they supporting what you want? What do their critics say? If you want to see new policies, write to your elected representatives and ask them what they are doing to change matters.

Shoppers also need to know enough about nutrition to ensure they buy foods with the ingredients essential for a healthy diet. When you read the label or buy fresh food, avoid items full of fats and sugars and go for those rich in vitamins. Vitamins are complex substances which can be found naturally in our food and which are vital to our health. We cannot make them in our own bodies and must get them from our diet or in synthetic form in pills. A well-balanced diet with plenty of fruit, vegetables, nuts, seeds, beans and grains, and maybe also fish, eggs and meat, should provide abundant vitamins which will help to keep you fit and healthy.

Rules for healthy eating:

1. Good food goes bad. Take care when buying and keeping food.
2. Eat healthy foods. Generally, those foods that are less processed are likely to be richer in valuable nutrients with good levels of dietary fibers.
3. No single food is entirely good or bad. It is the balance in a diet over the days and weeks which matters most. The only exception to this rule is the case of contaminated food - a single dose rich in salmonella or other bacteria can cause a severe attack of food poisoning.
4. Learn to be critical. Look carefully at labels. Ask questions and get the answers - you have a right to know about the food you are being sold.
5. Look for quality. If you can afford it, try buying foods which are better quality. But don't be too alarmed about problems like pesticide residues. It is better to eat lots of fruit and vegetables because of their valuable nourishment than to avoid them because of fears of any harmful effects due to chemical sprays.
6. When you buy chilled and frozen foods, make sure you place them in your own refrigerator or freezer as soon as you can. Make sure too that everything in your kitchen is stored at the correct temperature.

Glossary

Additives Food manufacturers have several thousand chemicals available to help change and improve the color, flavor, texture and shelf life of food. Most of them have little nutritional value and are used to make food appear more attractive than it would be otherwise.

Adulteration The quality of food may be lowered by adding cheap ingredients. Selling such inferior food as if it were pure is illegal, but there are many ways of legally debasing food: adding extra water, fat or fillers to meat products for example, or selling dilute fruit juice drinks as if they were mostly juice, or selling fish sticks which are less than half real fish.

Antibiotics Farmers who want to encourage fast growth and avoid any problems with sickness among their livestock may add antibiotics routinely to the animal feed. There are fears that residues may be in the meat we eat. Overuse of antibiotics encourages resistant types of bacteria to develop.

Carbohydrate This is one of three types of food energy (the others are fat and protein). "Simple" carbohydrate is sugar, "complex" carbohydrate is starch. Labels that just show carbohydrate values do not help us judge the amount of sugar, which we might want to avoid.

Contaminants These are unwanted and potentially harmful substances in our food, and include residues from pesticides, heavy metals in fish and antibiotics and hormones in meat. Additional contamination comes from microorganisms, like *salmonella*, which can give us food poisoning.

Dates (shelf-life) Most processed food is marked with a date showing the last day on which it should be sold (sell by) or the last day for eating (expiration date). There is usually a safety margin, and anyway, the dates have no legal status – it is legal to sell food after its sell by date. (It is illegal, though, to sell food unfit for consumption.)

Fat Fats and oils are one form of energy we can get from food. Certain types of fat (polyunsaturated) contain essential fatty acids which we need for brain cells, the heart and other organs. Saturated fat, on the other hand, is linked to heart disease and cancer. Good sources of polyunsaturated fats are the non-tropical oils (for example, sunflower, soy, corn) and oily fish (for example, sardines, herring, mackerel).

Fiber Dietary fiber is the part of the food found in most plant material which the intestine cannot absorb. It has a useful role in keeping the intestines healty, but high levels of fiber can reduce the amount of nutrients we can absorb.

Hormones Depending on a country's regulations, farmers may have a range of hormones available to boost the growth of their livestock. Hormone residues in meat are a cause of consumer concern.

Minerals Some minerals are essential in our diet. Iron, calcium, potassium and many others are essential for healthy body function. Good sources of minerals include vegetables, nuts, eggs, fish, lean meats and wholegrain foods.

Starch This is the more complex form of carbohydrate. It is the main form of energy found in vegetables like potatoes and carrots, and in grains and legumes. Refined starches, extracted from the plant, have been stripped of much of the useful nutrients.

Sugar This is the simpler form of carbohydrate, which can be found naturally in fruits and some root vegetables and in sugarcane. In its refined form it has been stripped of most useful nutrients and represents "empty" calories.

Index